SEA LEVEL

SEA LEVEL

Angela Leighton

Shoestring Press

Typeset and Printed by Parker and Collinson Ltd.
Nottingham NG7 2FH
(0115) 942 0140

Published by Shoestring Press
19 Devonshire Avenue, Beeston, Nottingham, NG9 1BS
(0115) 925 1827
www.shoestringpress.co.uk

First Published 2007
© Angela Leighton
The moral right of the author has been asserted.

ISBN: 978 1 904886 64 8

Shoestring Press gratefully acknowledges financial assistance from
Arts Council England.

ACKNOWLEDGEMENTS

'News', 'Skimmer', 'New Year' and 'Quint at Great Court' were first published in the *TLS*, 'Flying Westwards: 2 October 2002' in *Poetry Review*, 'Cambridge: Winter' in *The Dark Horse*. 'Pond' first appeared in *The Shop*, 'A Strand' in *Thumbscrew*, while 'The Sound Mirror: Kilnsea', '4 am', 'Foghorn', 'Rainsong', 'At the Vet's' and 'A Tree Sculpture' all appeared in *Stand*. 'Harbour', 'The Diver', 'Over', 'Sky Light' and 'Seconds' were published in *Metre*, while 'Apartment: Fifth Floor' and 'Moorlands' first appeared in *The Reader*. An earlier version of 'Drifts in Rosedale' was published in *The Way You Say the World: A Celebration for Anne Stevenson*, compiled by John Lucas and Matt Simpson, Shoestring, 2003. 'Piano Tuner' was first published in *Speaking English: Poems for John Lucas*, ed. Andy Croft, Five Leaves Press, 2007, and 'Sonar' in *On a Bat's Wing*, ed. Michael Baron, Five Leaves Press, 2007. 'A Figurehead' was commissioned by Hull City Council for the erection of the Hull-Vik sculpture, *Voyage*, by Steinunn Thorarinsdottir, and first published by them. Grateful acknowledgements are made to the editors of all these publications.

To those friends and colleagues who read and commented on poems, both in the early and in the final stages, my warmest thanks.

While discovery is the fact,
Sea-skill and the way to find ...

Laura Riding

We would make a circle, and never reach a shore at all ...and we
would be drawn down into the darker world, where other sounds
would pour into our ears until we seemed to find songs in them ...

Marilynne Robinson

Contents

HARBOUR

From creel-pots' crochet, dumped networks of nets,
staggered crates, a trailer, bales of twine,
bits and knots and art and old sea stench
under the nightly floodlight's yellow halo,

saints' wrack, livings, rot, planking, buoys,
rounding guts of rope, oarlock, airlock,
with aquapac and VHF, and luck,
light, weather, balance, ebb, flow,

something draws us out beyond the jetty's
throw, its sea-sliced steps and stop, its checked
halt, systoles of dulse, litter, scum,
to falls of sea-room falling wide as we come.

A STRAND

Small waves fall over themselves, getting nowhere.
The blue's brimful, complete. It takes sky in.
Sans titre. A line, *simple.* Colour, steeper.

Here, at the edge such blueness tears like paper,
marks where one country ends, another starts,
spills and drags a white, uncertain border.

Why should we want to come so near, on land?
The day's warm sand accommodates live shapes,
odd hips and elbows, fitting reverse plans:

my five-point hand, the palm's exact depression,
shallows of arms, the valley of the skull,
flatlands, notch and cast of a spinal column.

Nearby, the blue dilates, puts out white claws.
We are the tip of something unexplored.
It comes quite near, sometimes. But mostly draws

a blind over and over. Land shelves, and goes
deeper to mountains no-one names or knows.
The level-headed sea saves us from those.

THE DIVER

The unbreathable space will take him in,
sea, pocket his body quickly out of the sun.
He will not disturb its perfect coherence,
its tooled surface,
classical, protean, wind-worked hair--
the blue fluting's optical illusion
of going, always, somewhere.

He will not break the way sea breaks
up, anyhow, in the ears of caves,
runs itself out in waves
over sand or shale.
He will not change its whispering way
of saying nothing: *shh, shh*--
suspiria, something *(listen)* thrown away.

It is colder than he is.
And suddenly slow, slower than heartbeats, tightens.
He will assume
its dress, address of lost constellations:
pisces, aquarius. It makes room in its roomlessness.
Slow, lightened guests will go down
curiously flowering, still restless.

Is it a blessing? The heavy element
shuts mouth and ears. He will not hear
himself speak, only the sea's interminable volumes.
Those, wherever they unfold ashore, encounter brakes--
and will not record,
except by the tiniest, risen margin,
the difference he makes.

OVER

Here where the slip to lightness starts to start,
    and sea scrambles the line of its retreat,
cliffs stand back, big steps from this to that,
    a crossing where we will not find our feet,

I catch the highlight of an otter's back,
    slick along the water, through and through,
taking the shape of the sea, diving in loops,
    a pliant clasp, hooked on all that blue.

MAD MAELRUBHA TO THE ISLANDS

And islands, see, are meant to be God's stepping stones,
and this is saint's weather, stepping off almost
to nowhere, stepping into the wind's messageless stream,
because those wailing wainstones are the way to go
straight to the heart, a ford into that fastness which,
however you look's outlying always, always out,
by inches, miles, hand's breadth, crow's flight,
mainlands never here but only islands thrown,
like dice, at each new move, sea's roundabout:
Eigg, Muck, Rhum, Sanday, Canna, Soay,
each a saint's small step from nothing, fast in a stream,
points on the chart of drowning, maps of dream--

or anywhere that weather drives in blinding mists,
Force 10, westerly, not for fishers but fishers of men,
and nowhere either nearer, further, islands ending
quickly in a skirt of sea, a kelpie lather,
each weathered, won peak scraggled down,
stripteased with raining light and distance, cloud and sun,
Sgurr Alasdair long gone, Sgurr nan Gillean too,
when nothing is to hand except the sea, like smoke
whisked up by wind, and blindness raining thick as dust
upon the only island that we know, man-sized,
boat-rocked, bedrocked, no, just rocked, see, to stand
in the catastrophic cradle of God's hand.

BIG WHEEL

Lonely, already, in the changed cold--
the altered stations where we seem
not two, suddenly, but no-one at all,
fallen away, ourselves beyond
the fair's torrid scare and show
where lights run out, and then the city--
dangled high as a Christmas bauble,
knocked, rebuffed, by air's kid glove.

Love, this moon's one jot says nothing--
staring over everything's shoulder,
mine, yours, our shambles of bone,
blurred tally of flesh and will
that paid for it all--£2 a go
into sheer loneliness, no-holds, fingers
crossed, crossed--for how will this
shuddering, slow unfalling stop?

PIANO TUNER

Who is this man who listens? whose fingers crouch and call,
spanning small frequencies: the tilt of a tremor, the nerve-

centre of a note that hangs on nothing but itself? What
is the measure of this palpable reach, temper, touch-listening,

as if an ear to an ear could suddenly hear itself ring,
and crosswired lyric run, on air, easy as anything?

One, by one, by one, from nuts and bolts, from tacks,
strings, wrest-pins, by force, by hand, he draws each note,

sussing it out, from tusk, tree, root-nerve, growth-rings,
each jointed rod's retort, knee-jerk reaction, hammer-

blows' softened blows like news delivered gently.
Is it an entry to the underworld? Is it the soul?

Or workers' things, articulate joinery, bone and skin,
toolkits of hand, brain, ear--willing bodywork?

The bolted string shivers in its pin, biassed, taut.
A sound hangs in the hang of it. It fills the room,

as if a ghost has come again, in parts, in pieces,
frequent, keeping appointments with us, visiting.

I listen in. Spirit of anvil, hammer, stirrup,
moving spirit--somewhere, far back, we feel by it:

that tuning, wrench to true, a hand's reflex,
the pitched tremor of a branch the bird has left.

IN YOUR SKIN
(for Imogen, new-born)

You never tried it on yet it fits--
pink caul, birthday wrapper,
complete with prints, footprints, fingerprints,
all the necessary unread writing,
Rosetta stone or herringbone.
Look, it is your very own
   nerve coat.

Dear, it will grow on you.
Yours to keep warm or cold in,
see you through thick and thin.
You're touched in it--open to all
comers, shut in. You are your self's
foundling, gathered surprise and call--
   writing on the wall.

ALL SOULS

Let them come in.
Let those who gave up the ghost
put it, for one night, on.
Tonight they'll need a coat
against the cold within.

FOGHORN

Tonight the trees will not come home.
Revised, absorbed in a quilt of air,
their puzzled static might appear
anywhere, down streets or skies
   not known before.

Whiteness bluffs past darkened windows.
Half the street cuts out and leaves
light abstracted in the eaves.
Astigmatic roofs decline
   on clouds beneath.

Tonight the trees will not return.
Only a search-note in the brain
plies, like pain, its monotone.
No, no - - I dream the dead
   must phone, and phone.

MOORLANDS
(i.m. Kenneth)

Along what lines to call or seek to know
so much of nothing here? not metaphor
but geometry, earth's easy intersections,
planes, angles, lengths, and lengths to go:

a road for emphasis, the beck for wit,
the hills' running strokes, their post-impressionist
thicks of colour, summarising shadow.
Here's a land in outline, cut to fit.

It parts long hills from sky, a larch from stone,
and in the field-gate's rickety leger-lines
retains a smudge of wool, a ghostly ball,
minimal, like the shading of an O.

Dead or alive we say, and draw a line.
It takes a kind of pressure either side,
a hair's breadth, say, a spidery aural thread,
a gate (five fingers) throwing tunes to the wind.

Suppose these empty lines could hold your stare
hefted to this place, the moment's creature--
suppose I draw you back between the lines,
and make a note, an airy signature,

the catch of what might pass by any day--
will you be bound, perhaps, and stay? apply
yourself, a sense, a listening strain, attend
to where a place might sing -- like wind in a gate?

POETRY READING
(i.m. Michael Donaghy)

If I went back I'd see exactly where
he placed each word along a line of air
between St John's Wort and an ash (an ash),
pegging it in time, and temporarily
making a point, to weigh the lightness of it,
check its start, report, and let a pause
send the quiet out in all directions.
If I went back, I'd hear how poems talk.

MEMORIAL WILLOW, BUDAPEST
(i.m. Miklós Radnóti)

Call
a spade a spade
a bone a bone
a name a name
no-one's person.
This is a garden. Nothing grows.

What other news from underground
shows twinkling elvers in the late day's sun?
Each metal soul's flicked identical
tag adds its windfall token,
sum of silver, throwaway
name or number, links of mail.

Composed tree,
fountaining on groundless ground,

tributary,
a chandelier, with nerves of steel.

Chained rain
falls through each addressed leaf,

saving their names,
their dates (refrain), the same destination:

'45
or '44, blow by blow,

each leaflet's cold,
hammered silver. Willow willow.

This is a garden.
Nothing grows. And grows.

MARZABOTTO, 1944

Nothing

    to be said

nothing

    in your mouth

taste it

    (here

where lives

    went out)

nothing

    to be said

where nothing

    turns

in a pit of words

    to nothing again

        and again

            and

PEAT

It comes tight-packed, unearthly heavy, fat
with itself, intact. Handled, it crumbles to bits.

I sift and slip a landscape through my fingers,
feeling the way of forests, sun and rain,

trees that lean with the wind, that breathe with it,
and shake a hair of needles to the ground--

a plan of rusty crosses sinking in,
the wood's crossed fingers teasing out the sun.

Whose land is this? assorted, dry as dust,
evacuated of its lights and rains,

yet springy still, as if just stepped-off, live,
on some bare hillside subject to nothing but weather.

Its crumbs fall through my hands. I own the stuff,
its solving composition, settled dross,

the earth grown poor from forests it has lost.
This bit of unsoiled land is on my hands:

the bog's muck-sweat, hill-weathers' heavy loads,
the ways of ownership, those famine roads.

ROCKFACE

Far's as near as you get. It's close.
The fault's sheer--self in the act of itself,
a step from falling.

Imagine how high. No ties almost--
only the rock's coldly tethering flaws,
its cracks, lifelines,

on which you knot a hold halfway,
yourself for minutes on end
going nowhere,

above pure fall, vivid and breaking,
skirts of it, the slipknot names,
falls, fells,

losing their grip, landing a landslide,
the slate scree sheering away.
Here you're up

against it: stone's microscopic scratchwork,
manuscripts of weathering.
Close thing.

SKY LIGHT
(for Anne Stevenson)

Something early hesitates out there,
squares up, shows the roof's weak place.
A thin skin of glass lets in
visible greyness, 4 a.m.,

insists like anything, comes close up
against the guarded dark I slept in,
wins a desk back, table, chairs,
from where they went, yet still reserves

something secret as it comes,
formally, in time, to light--
dawning squarely like small sums:
a room, a date, a sheet of daylight.

SONAR

Dusk flushes the last light out   and sprouts
a bat,   flibbertigibbet, twitchy as nerves,
a phoning flicker, radar-singer.   And airy

as air, quick as a wink,   this flittermouse,
chamois leather,   dodges back, and back,
in a flap.   It calls each fact, maps the sound

of each obstacle thing.   Busy musician,
twittering wavelengths,   you make quick shapes
in your ears, you hear   the size of everything.

And we, in the half-dark,   sonar-sounded,
are noted also,   modulated
like stones and trees and walls.   We're all

ear-shapes, sound-ghosts,   plucked frequencies
drawn from the shadows.   This is the stuff
you sing by, steer by,   audible, avoidable.

Listen. Don't move.   Our dialled echoes
are pitched exactly   in another perspective,
tapped like rumours,   quickly transmitted.

Tiny busker, mathematician,   your flight
shirks matter lightly,   puzzles our physics.
Take your bearings.   Keep your distance.

This phoned world comes over and over,   micro-
soundings in the ear's soundboard.   Listen close.
It's thick with music,   answeringly tuned.

NEWS

Something about the way this melon gives
in to a knife, then rocks apart in halves,
its flesh pink and secret and surprised,
wadding round a slung hammock of seeds
that lifts easily, intact, a seating arrangement
for some blind, sudden-slow destination,
leaves me holding its packed, stored plan
for living, heavy, a moment, in both hands.

CITY

Why should we miss the trees?
Slow gardeners,
standing early as Easter
in parks, in streets--
why should we miss their feel
for what lies beneath?

their grip, knotted to earth's
reverse and dark,
a stillness still spreading
upwards, down--
their heads above, their purpose
underground.

Why breathe more freely wherever
they vary the air?
leave winter fingerprints
or summer hair?
Such formal brinkmanship's
an opening, anywhere.

HOTEL

I pay, then climb into the night's room.
A number tells me where I am
at home. I'll not remember soon.

Outside, there's too much light to dream.
The city's talkative. Sirens scream
in fifths, tuning. Here I'm clean

out of it, free. It lays no claim
to me, my unfound hiding, name,
the puff breath makes. I am the same,

but stranger, keen. I start to learn
my whereabouts by rote, short-term:
a bed, a room, a night, by turn.

Outside, the sky must save its skin.
It lets whatever the room keeps in
out in waves. The wall's too thin.

This night my numbered door might win
a lottery, stop an angel, summon
what lies open out there to come in.

4 AM

Why from so far back does guilt insist
on sour, thin ghosts sweating in corners?
Waking between the daylight and lost sleep,
I am my own deadweight, an aftertaste
of what, before, I never meant to say
but stays, half-true, half-seen, between
the living daylight and a losing dream.

It gapes, grips, squab thing, hungry
comeback, feeling for its life, for me,
a bird shape breaking out of my mouth,
the body of a wish, regret, a breath
expressed, its dusting on cold glass,
so that my own distaste tastes what it owes:
word, for word. And then cock crows, and crows.

DRIFTS IN ROSEDALE

The chimney's throat, fire-eater, cracks with heat.
A flame, small phoenix, arbitrates
its shrinking base,
tiptoes across the oxygenated rose,
skips a skinny cover of white ash
and eats the heart out of these coals.

It dodges up the wind-sipped flue, slips
live roots. A candle to dark drifts, it starts
to lose its grip,
give up the supple gold of its own ghost
for icing fields and skies alight with cold.
Imagine, dear, how near we come to those.

Up there, the railway's disused track might be
a tear, a scar-- faulting the hillside's
easy slide
from sky to dale. Its stepped, cut shadow
goes as far, almost, as Consett coalfields.
Here, old drift-mines tunnel into hills.

But drifts, tonight, are only ours and the snow's.
It brushes up the north side of stone walls,
fattens onto
leats and culverts, kilns and sidings,
badgering the hills until
its windfall hides whatever lurks below.

This chimney cools. Smoke twists--its upshot still
a signal of those rough descents
by drift or pit.
The huddled ash caves in. The lightened
clinker starves. My chimney shaft
cuts to dark--an ear to the heart of the hills.

MARGINALIA

These stalled waves of white leave
    a margin of quiet,
albumen to the words' quick,
ear to the sea, shell to a chick.
    The line's tectonic.
Either's both, a box-and-cox fit.
Hear, accept, a margin of error.
    Steer by it.

SECONDS

Odds 'n Ends, Bits 'n Bobs, Rag Bone--
my ball-and-chained self and shadow stop
short in bargain sunshine, down a knockdown street
of leaning fridges, suites, used beds, sunk chairs,
to say 'hallo' again to Jake's macaw,
perched just inches short of the open sky.

I say *hallo* in English. He looks sharp,
sideways, blinks a glaringly obvious eye.
A costume face flashes its maquillage,
crosspatch, pagliaccio, eyelined like a mask.
He flaps unhandy wings and feels for sky.
Those feathers sift a sunset, sift, revise.

Then quickly upside down (I am antarctic),
four wrinkled toes hook. He cocks
a look, shifts, adjusts, then turns art deco,
stiff as the florid handle of a jug, painted
curio staring from below. *Hallo,* I cadge,
and second-guess the thing he sees I am.

He's doubtful, climbs upright, hops his chain.
Then open-mouthed, unrolls a hingeing tongue,
shy, glossy mollusc shivering back,
and gags, and gags, unwraps a mouthful, something
hard-won, brought to light, precise *bon mot:*
Fuck Off, the bird calls, wondering still, aloud.

DEGREE CEREMONY

How faces come by air, or land, or water
to themselves, by years, by centuries,
by grace and chemistry, three thousand million
years to here, a sea flows to a hall.

So channelled water flowers from its own flow,
superfluous, a fountain cut to curb
the lit, runaway angel in its skin.
Water goes. A carved fall holds.

And in these faces, relayed like still waves
from other faces, redisposing their split-
second looks in queued-for, crowded eyes,
a log of lives flow-charts the look they keep.

By water, by repeats and tallies, hand-
me-down helix, engineering feats
of frowns and smiles--this ninety percent soluble
self's a short time-piece. We inherit the sea,

its fall, still. Over the face of the waters,
by slow degrees, by chlorophyll, blue-greens,
by simple, complex cells, our faces come
strangely, precisely here, full to the brim.

DUSK CHORUS

Because at dusk's slow dimmer-switch
  a pause turns on
the sound of something so surprised,
  we call it song--

and sing is what we say, to ease
  the thought of what
sickness, rage, or hunger feed
  a bird's technique.

ANOTHER COUNTRY

The still terror of a hare seems earthenware.
Sky revises light to anywhere.

One field's a knitted brown, two-ply, three-ply.
A fence has wired it in. (So fields must lie).

A mapping kestrel cuts a wider flight,
describes a looser tether out of sight.

A birdwing cuffs the hedge. The herd's shy swerve
tap-dances fear, heart-in-their-feet, root-nerve.

I'm news, not good, for skin on tenterhooks
of spine or haunch. So, radio'd in their looks,

their early-warning ears, their feelings' stare,
I stand accused: I'm freely standing here.

FLYING WESTWARDS: 2 OCTOBER 2002

Feast of All Angels that fly by day,
by daylight's lightweights, cirrus-floored,
a white lagging in the world's roofspace,
and soul, a microlite or boeing,
nosing through a blue bend,
tilting a shoulder-bladed wing
to weightlessness, no-holds, some going's
sheer precarious openness and cold.

Imagine an angel come to light.
Its glass skin adjusts sunshine
to intravenous blue. It is exacting,
full also, as angels are,
of the bright capacity of nothing.

Light-headed light, a lens reversed,
our watch stopwatched, not clockwise wise,
the soul's acrostic lost in sky's
round trip, pure optical hazard,
stinting the minutes we mark, then hours--
sun and wing like God and Adam,
in the beginning.

A sweepstake blue takes all we are,
eyebright, cup of unconsummated summer,
sun-trap, unendurable verandah--
sky letting
whatever warmth the earth breathes, out,
making light,
in the turned jar's almost-nowhere,
of what we were, love, under the heavens above.

POINTS

That moon's so ripe it will soon fall out of the sky.
The garden holds a wedding and a wake.
This eye's an addict, hooked
on how pure white
fires

whatever pallid stone or flower it finds.
Nothing romantic here, more like
an ossuary come to light,
a glamour earth
excites.

Imagine how white unripens everything back,
chalks the world we're in, all things
missed and pure and thin,
and moon the point
of nothing.

The valley's V is quarter filled with sea.
Chalkwhite's too live by half.
Marble or bone shines under the grass
like moonlight trickled out-- soft stuff, ground down,
but hard enough, walking, when you see
brightness like a flashpoint in the earth.
It seems a thing you know, nails, teeth,
a terra firma beached up on itself.
1941, what do we know?
seas' cretaceous wrack beneath our feet.

These green seersucker fields extend as far
as the last Downs' arses, then the cliffs.
No chance those planes will miss
their blanched cross-section, Seven Sisters,
seven sleepers under their sheets,
or Beachy Head, that baldy, thrust
up from an old continental fault.
(Always there's a noise in my head).
Chalkwhite's too live to see.
History, too sad to live.

I was always the problem, cut
on the bias, the cross,
throwing its shadow, struck by itself,
myself's stalker, interrupter.
But this is worse, this gleam in the earth,
white threads, shocked hair,
small creatures ground down, one by one:
snails, ammonites, coccoliths, clams.
Chalkwhite's too live, or dead.
Now, 1941.

LEAVINGS

It says something,
wind-somersaulted litter, shushed into corners,

morning-after
gasps of dirty chip-bags, wrappers, carriers,

shiny or drab,
lettered in fast colour, absent content.

It touches on
this and that, whispers along the street

sweet nothings,
groundswell of airiness, fancy flights,

and turns in a wheel
of the wind, footworks the gutter, dervishes

to drains and ruts,
airbricks, breaks, gaps, shafts, sudden

dips of upper
into underground. A sybilline

shuffle, scrapped
leaves, ways, invitations, way-

laid, late
emptiness trails us, staying apart, behind.

TWO WOMEN

Each knows enough.
It's in the air, shy as a cat's back,
thrilled like a drawn rope, knotted lash,
the worry beads of a prayer, but not to touch.

It is transmitted.
Sensory fibres fork their lightning quick
to the dreamed claw in the air, grappling with it.
Something electrifies by being not there.

What is it? Where?
Thought's ghost, hanging on nothing, on each
word, cherry-picked, quick, and snapped clean
from the branched tree of every stretched nerve.

So where were we?
Light vacates the room and goes right
round the other side of the world. Here, inside,
each word's moon shines, in a little sky.

I estimate
the listening lie of a cat, its technical
panache for sleep, the tail's smile tidied
beside a shell-shape, sea purring in it.

RAINSONG

You know the rain by each car's shushed repeat,
that rising scale, that raring to go quiet.

Tyres tread an aquaplane, like *yes-s-s,*
yes-s-s, the sense, in time, diminishing

to just a guess, a wish or hint--breath
(its disappearing trick), still practising--

so distances, arranging like a phrase,
rise and fall, coming, going away,

until that pause--: nothing again to hear,
and rain, sheet-music, hanging in the air.

SUSPENSION

Humber drags mud feet in the sun,   lazes round
     its old easy ground, feels
               the rut it's in   and
pulls its weight
          through and through a length, tail-
endish,
     running out of itself,
              easy to this.

It saps hills,
       distills
   sky colour from sky,
         crumbles, slides.
              And shoves
silt, muck, wood, scrap, chemical effluence,   then
       conjures a spill,
scales its own departure,
        snags
         downhill.

What takes the flow so lightly here and stays
     bobbing?
       snarled on itself,
the trick of it danced
      on what runs away?

A slack bolt,
               sash of rain
                              sliproads its going, over-
runs a standstill and
                             commutes endlessly
under the curved phrase of a bridge.

It might be the easiest thing on earth.

A line, a join,
               stepped out
                             on arch and stress,
on steel   concrete   asphalt   lead
               the lightest instep   step-
                                  ing,
                                      first-
                                          footing
                                                  itself.

APARTMENT: FIFTH FLOOR

Steps in the street, in the small hours, go
streetwise in twosomes, tic, tac,
in 2/2 time or else 2/4.
The scratch of a heel, upbeat, then
tiptoe, feels its way to a door--
a lit auditorium of walls, all ears,
catches a quickness, a fear, sometimes
the vast indecision, is it? of a pause.

Who is abroad? What stops in its tracks?
In the gods I half-sleep. Stars shift
their usual scenery, digital, crystal.
The city's acrid thermals rise.
Something is out, a secret, a step,
taking its time. Quietness texts
a heartbeat, breath, sounding the wide
open loneliness cities keep.

SNOW AT CAFÉ LATTITUDE

Something changes the rain's mind, gives pause, finds
another way to fall aside.
A polka dot design alters, crosswise, on light.

My cupped hands round a capuccino
(monkshood, bone cowl)
hug for warmth.
Gravity
takes a moonwalk in the kingdom of light.

Snow's on air. Its curtain fall
is falling starting everywhere, who knows? so
a lightly floored whiteness loads
the kerb's granite, snub-noses cars,
crusts the shape of what's forgotten, layer by layer.
Snow's white cosy winters everywhere.

And dashed grey rain hatches crystal like wit.
Thermodynamic
angels bat their spotted wings, make
a flurry
under the lit amazement of the lamps.

My hands hug
bone china, bone. (It's going cold.)

This monk, hoodie, cooped, cupped.
A joke. But.

Cold at heart,
each blown flake's antlered star is
quashed, unmarked.

GREENHOUSE, WITH CACTI

What lies between something ... and itself?   Paul Valéry

Always just on the other side of here.
Go quietly now. Don't knock or ring.

Don't think or turn, or try to run.
Enter the sun's angled lens,

a section of air, adjusted by glass,
like Arizona turned out, inside,

and easily missed. Look, it's packed
with light to the rafters, light to the hilt,

a turn between what's out and in.
Go carefully. Cross the dimension

of pure indifference. Imagine the same
again, apart, a glass partition,

perhaps a house of cards, criss-crossed,
like girdered air. It's not too far

to these things, bristling, inching up,
their prickly hosiery fat with filling.

Theirs are such slow hopes *(don't touch)*,
fists set at an unreachable heaven.

Centuries pack and swell their gooseflesh,
fleck with grey, vegetable hairs

their anguished limbs, their poking aims.
Cross the dimension, call it love.

They have no roots, but yearn obtusely,
thumbs-up, butting into light,

or kinky, suddenly bent drain-pipes.
The sun's lens keeps them to it,

intensified, set aside from us,
though cut sky's as clear outside,

and weather looks identical
from either side of where we stand.

Come. Enter the hall of desires,
step across the line that marks

what lies between something and itself.
Note the change, gauge the interval.

Like touching glass, F sharp, G flat,
the limma of a difference that

quirks the set of where we are:
for here, elsewhere, light-years, a star.

COUSIN BUTCHERS
(for Cesare and Sergio)

They are the gentlest handlers, almost shy.
They can sense rawness, feel for where it felt,
touch, like insight,
something oddly sculptured on the shelves.
They know the layout of its tenderness.

Like subtle geographers, they read terrain.
And follow marbling contours, printed faults,
the rosied section that must mean
it bled.
They're connoisseurs of how it gives and falls.

This is a strange stall, cool, open to the street.
Its puzzling bestiary
is visible, all inwardness on show:
hearts, lights, livers, brains.
There are white ropes, pink stacks, unnerved, named.

No flinching. That's all done.
Something has withdrawn into these facts.
They lie with such abandoned purpose here,
landscaped on trays, like sudden,
rare colourists of what lies hidden in us.

Family, too. No getting away from that.
The shivered ballet of their herd-taught nerves,
fear's ancient footwork, sharp, concerted, learned,
swerving, haunts our eyes.
He lifts the thing and softly asks: how much?

LOTTO'S CAT
(from 'The Annunciation')

Then that *thing*! Visitant, spirit, what have you,
bird-creature misting up the room,
like bad weather.

This one freaked me, coming up behind,
shocked through my coat and claws,
stopped me, mid-walk, prickling my skin.

Not that I saw anything, mind--
the quiet, as usual, things in their place,
her hand lifted in surprise, like *hallo*.

I never cared for it, *seeing* things--
the room not quite as roomy as before
but thick and speaking--

an interference, empty air
birthing itself.
I think I smelt it, fishy, behind me,

this un-creature, out of its skin,
like nothing roused, a suffered turn,
worse than unborn.

What would she want with it, coming in
unasked, unknown, angling there
among tables, chairs?

Not that I heard anything, mind,
just the quiet, exercised.
It sounded like the saddest of stories.

That girl never moved.
Nothing good will come of it, be sure--
neither fish nor mouse.

DONATELLO'S DAVID

Here's a one. Nothing on,
but knee-high gaiters and a cocked hat.
Pin-up boy, out for fun.
That big fella? Knocked 'im flat.

THE PRISONERS

Caro m'è 'l sonno, e più l'esser di sasso   Michelangelo

How shall we bear it, these blocked imaginary feet,
hands gloved in the earth's unforgiving crust--
half-formed, half-known, intaglio, rock art, stone,
a clamp of matter closing round our hopes?
Will someone chisel the asking lie of our limbs,
crack the stump of this founding paralysis--

and bring us to term, to light, groomed and finished?
Our metamorphic shapes are ghosts of stone.
Fast in the marble's cold anatomy, heavy
at heart, our mineral blood stops at the start.
We cannot lift a hand or force a foot.
Landlocked -- in us life's gravity cries out.

POND

My net drags weed, slime, leaves,
hairnet of duckweed, brown web, grabs
a winter salad, threads of green—

and then scoops death: a white heaviness
queered by the water's restless pulse,
a blurred bubblewrap hugging round,

till something comes unclear and starts
to fall to bits in air that takes
a hand, I sense, in finishing it.

I retch, step back. *How did a rat?*
This wild catch is not what I looked for.
Leaking through the straining mesh

is soluble fact, a mess of rat-foot,
rat-tail, all the intelligent head--
the rest, ribboning out of itself.

And all I can think is how soon matter
deserts itself, a runaway trick,
becoming almost nameless already—

the rat absolved of rat, the foot
of running, something of having to live
up to itself. Now it can

unshackle its rat joins, relax, finally
give itself over to air's pickings,
spread, to rest--

here, where I pitch it quickly in,
holding my breath. The muddling soil's
familiar rut accepts the gift.

★ ★ ★

Later, white lilies will float a tea-set,
skin-deep, clear-cut, on the water's flat,
and keep their day's appointment with the sun.

That cool blaze recalls, re-tells
a wish long buried in a book of tales:
the dead, once met among the asphodels.

45

AT THE VET'S

On my hands--
the life's small patter and fall, tail's anger,
radio rod of the bone, follicle, hair's-breadth whisker,
        lover, killer,
all the shadow stuff of the given-up creature.

She'll go lighter
in and out of our thoughts all day, for what's left
lying quietly behind on a table, simpler-seeming:
        old coat
dropped in a hurry, too heavy, like fur in summer.

SONG FOR THE ICE MAN
(for Robert)

Did weather turn winter one September
before Septembers even existed?
Did winds change course and snowstorms gather,
quietness fall clearer than ever?

Did skies confuse and paths disappear,
the night swing shut like a death-trap door,
and fifty centuries open their story,
five thousand years perma-frost your hair?

Dear fellow, lost beneath each summer
with copper axe and belted tinder,
boots and hood, leggings and fur--
disclosed unknown, time-stopped time-traveller.

This deep preserve of cold is yours,
its keep and mould, its long procedure.
Lonely hunter, glazed warrior,
ice your storer, restorer, lover,

heart-stopper-- what do we know?
The sudden wide snow, altered
waymarks, ancient faults and fissures,
zero, sub-zero, still going under,

until, one day, the ice-cap's far
melt unpacked you from your crystal lair,
divulged a stiff, familiar figure--
history's guy, keeper's joker.

CAMBRIDGE: WINTER
(for Stefan)

The river's curbed bent
                    invented a city.
Its flourish meant
                    weather, meant tiny
deflections of soil, meant
                    founding a living,
signing the routes of stones,
                    cornering
a place to stay their weight,
                    and leave them standing.

King's Chapel lifts   like grasses singing,
fluted, reedy,   cropped from the fens' washed flats,
sedge-thin,   its stems of stone, its blown blades,
panpipes or wicker   pared, and instrumental.

It is strip-willow,   pillars like wicks of rushes
scored upright   from the lodes and dug channels.
It is   flood plains in flower, trimming heaven,
carex, calamus,   windlestraw on the common.

Or,   like stone osiers ranged in rows,
all   filigree high-rise, all echo.
Cold, minutely combed sky   closes
round   tipped poplars, coppiced willows.

I stand counting: twenty-six spindles catch
woollens, silks.   (Twenty-six letters fill
billions of books.)   A squirrel suddenly brush-
strokes a branch, monkeys   hands-and-tail, goes

flinging on a high career, then   cartoons
running.   Sky enquires the point of everything.
It seizes shapes,   carves the napkin-ply
of a swan,   the tiny spires of green lawn.

I practise sanity.   Spring's coiled syllable
stays shut   on the tongue. It puzzles the future.
Singing   cuts like masonry chisels, high
and clear.   Ancient willows justify the river.

QUINT AT GREAT COURT

I am lost above these lands,
　　in star spaces, ambiguous haunts,
seeing the rights of overlord
　　or seignory of what we are:
scholar, bedder, beadle, don.

　　I overlook myself from here
in small battlements, allotted rooms,
　　and see a ghost in the interval--
a quintessential shape that makes
　　demur between what is . . . and is,

like points, ellipses lost for words,
　　cursors running the screen's blank page.
I am itself . . . its self, the way
　　a figure dreams of being dreamt--
nothing you'd know, not done or said,
　　but fallen free, between, by the way.

LOUGH BRAY

This cold eye sees what is going.
Weather-wise, in the bone of nature,
in a crux of hills,

its brainless lens accepts what comes.
Come, see how seeing might be done:
no nerves, no words,

the *macula lutea* of
a lovers' tryst, daylight as clear
as day, as light,

and sky pooled in a cruet of earth,
blue or grey, bright or dark,
a matching sight

that cannot hear the skylark's reel
harass the air, or catch the wheatear's
flashing arse--

liverwort, liverfluke, sheep's dip, lamb's ear,
gipsy stuff, or even us,
standing apart,

looking across its eye-to-eye
in a cross-purpose nothing can adjust,
or simplify.

BY LIGHT-YEARS

Is it a kind of grief?
a double-stopping song or two-part piece
that shows the strain, the widening gauge between
    two facts in time:
this second of attention, called myself,
that pricking light already out by years?

My senses stream in lines,
in tiny straight counts of days and hours.
Out there, the zone is round. A memory,
    not mine, unfolds
its star-shapes in my simple-seeing eyes,
exacts, long gone, long dead, points in the sky.

What tense am I? what time?
How does the grammar of a sentence start to ply
light-years? or stand for what's divulged long after
    it dies? How bend
my words to absent brightness, tease a fact
out of the dark's prehistory, to now?

If grief, it's pure, not applied.
There's nothing here but the maths of speed and light,
the flowered sum of driven, violent power,
    quintillion night.
It seems too far to count, a fantasy
of point no point, a shifting chart of fires.

And I, tensed and timed,
must miss what lies in leap-time, speeds along
in ultra-sound, an apogee in the curving
    variables of light.
My messenger senses probe the night's archive:
Sputnik, Mariner, Magellan, Galileo, Enterprise.

I'm fast, in minutes of time.
My mind, sentenced to past and future, now
and after, to the largely insignificant accident
    of being here,
finds life, in the grip of the earth's tilted round,
a grief, a surprise, unappeasable, always applied.

SPURN

(The moving three-mile sand and shingle spit at the mouth of the Humber.)

1 A Figure

Something cries. Is it wind in your eyes?
Its fetch, salt-heavy, sand-spiked,
shouldering up the waves this side
of where we stand,
on banked boulder clay and shale,
chalk and flint spangling the shingle.

Or else, perhaps, it's sand in your eyes?
A crumbling outlook deals a hand
of tides, ords, blow-outs, groynes.
It must invent
this spit, index, appendix. Is it
a plank to stand? a way to be
at sea on shore, going nowhere?

Figure it, bit by bit,
the recomposition of a drift--
versatile in inverse sense,
like sand uphill, hard work, or else
a reflex from
the westering plexi-form of waves,
a landing-strip.

Imagine it
fantasy, mapmaker's wit:
Ocellum Promontorium,
Ravenser Odd,
a quirk or slip of the tongue, an old
fancy or skit
of the too grave, land-making god, bored of his fix.

So what is it?
Whiplash struck from terra firma,
whim or error,
snag, turning over and over,
a tongue or trick
of the sea's lingua-form, its murky
idiolects of weathering.

Consider, then.
The squat pin of a lighthouse stops
none of it going,
running aground, sifting over
its own departure,
drawing, year by year, along
the altering line it must draw after.

Notice how
sandwort, saltwort, storksbill, bindweed
root lightly,
knot their lives on makeshift, landshift,
catching on it--
twists on the moving dump of slack,
ties in the wind's switched carelessness.

See, now.
Figure an open way to know.
Risk how it goes.
This fools' sand slides under our feet.
A tenuous length of land runs out,
and we, unbound,
are walking on the ghost of ground.

2 Telling the Time

The clocks all out--
too late already or too soon struck,
they wave from times
of their own devising.

Two fingers to us--
out by several degrees.
Little wonder, dear.
Was it days or years?

3 Quick

Happy as a sandboy, hautboy, water-
slipper, whippersnapper (hey,
not so fast)--
a handful, tearaway,
afoot in the bloodflow,
                    breath-stop, lymph-run,
coming in
the wink of an eye, the grip of a hand,
a dance on the machair,
                    entrechat, chassé and
(tap, tap), slippy.

What is the quick of this quicksand?

4 Skimmer

Halfway between salt water and fresh,
tidal and still, blue light, blue wet,
are sandbanks where a man jet-skiied,
then walked between the sky and sea,
himself's horizon running out,
fitful ellipis, stabbing a thin line.

I skimmed a stone that told its own
scansion, hurried faster over
stone's deadweight, till water opened
up to it. Density wins.
A thickness sends us under, quick,
unless, as quick, we skim.

5 Groynes

A cold sea overturns, overturns.
Sand's too subtle to keep. It goes.
A spit of land
inches tidewards under the groynes'
pinning hold, their rickety stitching.

Blackened legers, driven stakes,
keyed in rows at the edge of the world,
leaning to Force 9, Force 10, still
in marching order from a long-finished war.
Why do they look like trees walking?

The longshore drift catches at their feet.
Wind rakes them like a field of tombs.
Badged by nails, fishnet, weed,
they stand to something in the air, the air,
purposeful, obscure,

like listening posts in the wind's Kaddish,
whisperers, bowed down, in the know.
Why do they seem to carry heavy loads?--
out of kilter
on their long road, coming to the water.

Gaunt pointers, dug in, waiting--
they might underpin the land's slow shift,
shore this spur
of till, shingle, boulder clay,
fend against the fetch of waves.

But not for long.
Anonymous mourners on the losing side,
telegraphs of no-one's news,
they might wear weather like a habit now.
Why do they still darken the day's view?

6 Currents

Greedy Gut. Stony Binks. Old Den.
                                Dear,
you must
                            give up, give up.
It swallows (you), a tit-bit, crumb,
                        morsel to munch.

A gulp of the drink it downs, you are
            blown in the storm's
                            gobbling contraflow,
            the wave's pulled face,
                        its funny mirror.

A loosening boy elongates as if,   lycra,
                            elastane,
        fools'   shape always coming into view.

I hold a hand out,   snatch what I can.

It runs to nothing,
                    slips

a sea through my hands.

7 Numbered

By rule, set, calculator, spreadsheet,
I, Phaedra, on the road's backbone
walk by rote of telegraph poles.
I, and I, and I, a yoke--
numbers hang on an empty line.

Hartburn, Monkwell, Colden Parva,
drowned names, mnemonic rounds--
a song for what the tide must take,
give an inch, a mile-- I, and I.
The gas terminals remember lost lives.

A count to countdown, out from the start.
Tide's a landgrabber, bit by bit,
and *psst, psst,* listen to it:
the gas jets shoot underwater,
hitting the wet, so much, so much less.

And I, Phaedra, on the road's backbone,
follow its concrete plate tectonics,
shifted and shocked, its fossil sleepers,
axial, columnar, skeleton ladders
sunk to shadow, nearly invisible.

I count and miss. Myself's just out.
I should add up, but is it so much?
I dream by numbers, multiplier
of summer, autumn, winter, spring,
clock myself up by minutes again:

one, and one, and one. Imagine
grass in the wind, grains in the sand.
My timed hand, numbered fingers,
all the skin's complex calculations,
log their graining, score their run.

And I, Phaedra, on the road's platform,
caught between North Sea and Humber,
add myself to the known sum:
one and one ...feeling the odds
that come, and come (between us), love.

8 New Year

So little light to spare.
The day's last stroke leaves
  a sense of rose.

No sooner seen, sundown
goes underground. And mud beside
  a river shows

tiptoes, treads, the arrow-
headed notes of how a seabird
  comes and goes.

9   Touches

Land turns in its cycles of sleep.
Sea lies awake.
Spurned, scaped, the shoreline they keep.

Toccata, a nerve that has to sing.
Fricative,
the sound of forces tampering.

As if the place, pure instrumental,
broke to repair.
The injuring air is musical.

This hand in hand, a shore. Now see
(finishing touches)
how finishing still touches me.

Facing nothing not here, it might take everything in:
batteries of waves, the fulmar's divebomb, sky's all-clear,
sand compiling itself in tiny heaps and falls,
a paperwork, dextrous wind, subsiding shore.

Who knows what it hears? a blank, concrete ear cupped
on air, eavesdropping zeppelins still--or else by a far
stretch of imagination, harriers, B-52s.
Who hears falling? Quiet breaks in the sound's mirror.

A TREE SCULPTURE

Is she mine, this turned, wooden mermaid,
bluntly levelled, cut and shaped,

twisted round a trunk not hers,
with bare ribs, groovy hair?

There's a look in her eyes that makes a stare.
She's staked, see. A suicide.

Or, stumped by ground, her earthed tail's
drawn to a temporary afterlife.

Imagine a style of being alive,
stiff and quiet, simplified,

not feeling rain, these cuffs of wind,
the owl's prolonged, sad solo,

hooey with night (woodwork, woodwind).
So something died, and yet remains.

And I, slipped out this windy night,
seeing the turned lathe of her ribs,

the rooted wave of her chiselled tail,
recall another night as if

a lifetime slipped--and touch, for fire,
dead heartwood pinned inside.

THE SAND CHILDREN
(for Peggy)

They seem to shoulder air with ease, these bony children,
buckling to, in sudden sharp Zs
on hassocked sand,
landing themselves on its slippery territory.

Tricked out of air, were they? into shins and elbows and knees,
hitched into limbs? a thin rigging of bone
underpinning
self's strange sense, its reach and ending.

That paper-pattern fragility's only ours, rearranged.
Consistencies survive and leave a print.
Shadowy,
as shale laminae layered in bedding-planes,

the understated, oscillating shoulder-blades,
gear-shifts behind the adept, flickering hands
that build, in play,
fragile, collapsing castles against the waves.

Children come like homing creatures here, sandlings,
still summering for a season, feeling the sea
repeat, revise
its long, slow breathing exercise.

Turning now, I see them only where, so far,
sea's fluent border shifts a weight.
Waves and dunes
absorb them, matter haunts them like a ghost.

Out of our hands, they are--so distantly composed,
cradled from air and water, quartz and schist--
children found
in the making of what goes, and has to live.

LIONFISH

You come into view, *courante*, in a flow like the sea's
tempo in colour.
Like nothing we know, though 'lion' tags your shape--
a price to pay
for the brilliant, peacocked, knife-pleated flare you are,
venomous, all frills,
and quick as a switch the fibre-optic lights
streaking in waves.
You're sea in a lit spectrum, a piece of its play.

As if light-years
had flexed you into changing colourfulness,
mixed a palette
of browns, blues, greens mid-stream, hung
haberdasheries:
spindles, lobes, fringes about your skin.
You're odd, accessory.
Invisible weather fans such scalloped wings,
fingers thin hems,
winnows the marbling wave of tail and fin.

Is it anger, that stare?--
the whiskered insect horns, leaf-wattle lips,
toy-tiger frown--
or carnival, association's tricks?
Such finery's
survival. You're a scare. And, bright as sunshine,
dressed to kill.

Through glass, through darkening water, worlds apart,
   you fluctuate,
a dream through moving sea's deflected field,
   a semaphore,
subtle as sea's glove-puppet through and through--
   the flex and pulse
of what we might imagine from the shore.
   Do waves' arranging
metronome of markings on the sand
   waver in you?

Lion, lionfish--your mimic, swimming wings
   might slip, catch,
the clear, cold frequency at which sea sings.

A FIGUREHEAD

(For the sculpture, Voyage, *on Victoria Pier, Hull)*

Hull, Immingham, Grimsby, Spurn--
in the set sun's spilt cordial
P & O's big ghost goes out
night after night, like the dead from home.

Here's a leaning of the spirit, drawn
out from upright, off from true,
a header into the wind, full-tilt,
the bent of going, at a stroke, stopped still.

Exchange and pact, sagas of return,
a sea-sickening in the ear's dark hold--
yet out, out, sea-farer, wanderer,
Njal, Unn, old comers and goers,

like birds that trade their lands each year:
whooper, diver, plover, eider,
sandpiper, snow-goose, tystie,[1] tern--
that urging back, that longing to be gone.

Is this the compass needle of the north
that sets the heart at ice and snow,
that draws toward its zero point,
and rocks our stand, unfathoms our roots?

Like *I*, in italics, this bowsprit figure,
clean as a sloping drift of snow,
looks out and shows how close we are,
how far, how cold, the last sea goes.

1   The Scottish name for the Black Guillemot, variations of which
are still used in the Faeroes and Iceland.